MAY YOU FIND COMFORT, JOY,
AND PEACE IN THE PROMISES OF GOD!

3558 S. Jefferson Ave., St. Louis, MO 63118-3968

1-800-325-3040 • cph.org

Manufactured in Dongguan, China \ 055760 \ 340854.

1 2 3 4 5 6 7 8 9 10 32 31 30 29 28 27 26 25 24 23

GOD'S PROMISES FOR ME

A BIBLE JOURNAL FOR KIDS

FOR ALL THE PROMISES OF GOD FIND THEIR YES IN [JESUS].

2 CORINTHIANS 1:20

HOW TO USE:

READ GOD'S PROMISES TO YOU. His Word is trustworthy and true. Memorize the Bible verses to keep God's promises in your heart!

Think about the way that God is keeping His promises to you. ***DOODLE AND JOURNAL YOUR THOUGHTS.***

DISCOVER HOW GOD KEPT HIS PROMISES TO PEOPLE IN BIBLE TIMES. Look up the Scripture passages to learn more about these Bible events.

SAY A PRAYER, thanking God for keeping all His promises in Jesus!

GOD'S PROMISES TO YOU:

I CREATED YOU AND YOU ARE WONDERFULLY MADE.

For You formed my inward parts; You knitted me together in my mother's womb. I praise You, for I am fearfully and wonderfully made. ***PSALM 139:13–14***

In the beginning, God created the heavens and the earth. In six days He created light, galaxies, mountains, oceans, and all kinds of animals—and He saw that it was all good. Then, God made the crown of His creation—people—and He saw that everything was *very* good.

READ ABOUT IT IN GENESIS 2:1–25.

DEVOTIONAL THOUGHT

God made you and He knows you completely—inside and out. You are exactly who He has created you to be! You are His unique and beautiful child. Draw a portrait of yourself in the frame below.

DEAR HEAVENLY FATHER,

I praise You that I am wonderfully made, by You! When it feels like no one understands, remind me that You love me and know me completely—inside and out. In Jesus' name I pray. **AMEN.**

I AM WITH YOU WHEREVER YOU GO.

Be strong and courageous. Do not be frightened, and do not be dismayed, for the LORD your God is with you wherever you go. JOSHUA 1:9

After Jacob tricked his father and angered his brother, he had to pack up and leave home. He felt alone and wondered what would happen next. God appeared to Jacob in a dream and promised to be with Jacob wherever he would go.

READ ABOUT IT IN GENESIS 28:10–22.

DEVOTIONAL THOUGHT

No matter where you go, God promises to be with you. Use your finger to trace the path through the labyrinth (maze) to the center of the heart. Try drawing your own labyrinth on a separate piece of paper. Write "Jesus" in the middle. Start by making a simple spiral. You can also look at the example here or online and create a more complex labyrinth.

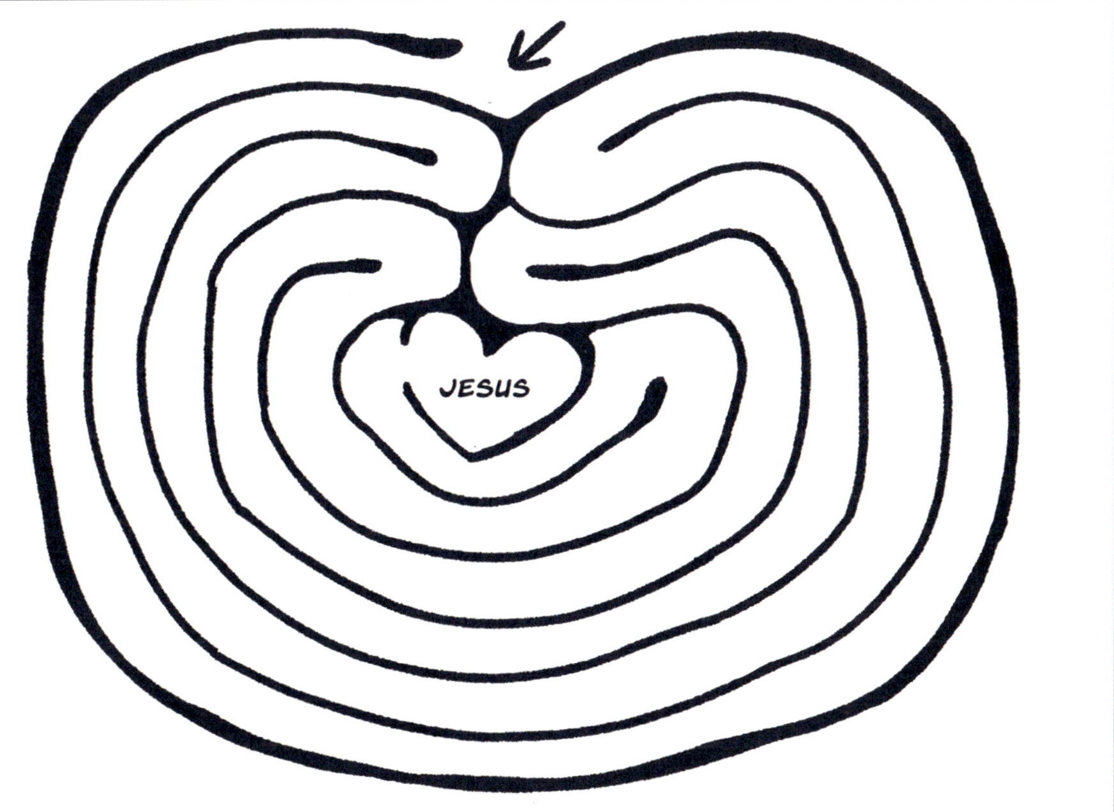

DEAR HEAVENLY FATHER,

Thank You for Your promise to be with me no matter where I go. When I feel alone and afraid, remind me that no matter what direction life takes me, You will always be right by my side. In Jesus' name I pray. **AMEN.**

I HAVE A PLAN AND A PURPOSE FOR YOUR LIFE.

For I know
the plans I have for you,
declares the Lord, plans for welfare
and not for evil, to give you a future and a hope.

JEREMIAH 29:11

Joseph's life was full of ups and downs, twists and turns. But through it all, he trusted that God was in control. God moved Joseph from favorite son to Pharaoh's second in command (and all the steps between) in order to save His people.

READ ABOUT IT IN GENESIS 37 AND 45.

DEVOTIONAL THOUGHT

God knows what is going on in your life. He has given you an identity and a purpose. You are His child, you are loved, and you are sent into the world to share His love with others! It's fun to think about what your life might be like when you are older. Fill in the blanks below with your thoughts. Remember that no matter what happens, God has a plan and a purpose for your life!

MY PLANS

Ten years from today, I will live in the country of ______________ in the town of _____________ with _____________ and my __________________. I will work as a _______________. I will often wear _______________. My favorite thing to do will be _______________. I will love ____________ and ______________, but I won't like _______________.

God's plans: He will be with you every day of your life, loving you and leading you.

Decorate the edges of this box with doodles of your life ten years from now.

DEAR HEAVENLY FATHER,

Thank You for Your promise to lead and guide me through life. When I doubt myself, remind me of my purpose and Your plan for me. Help me to show Your love to others. In Jesus' name I pray. **AMEN.**

I HEAR YOUR PRAYERS.

Before they call I will answer; while they are yet speaking I will hear. *ISAIAH 65:24*

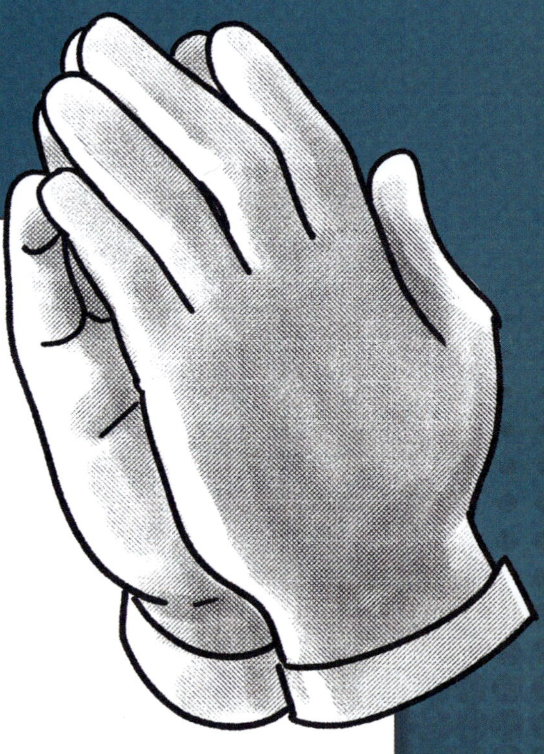

Hannah was sad. She didn't have any children. She prayed and prayed to God for a child. Do you think God heard her prayers? Yes, He did! When the time was right, God gave Hannah a very special baby boy.

READ ABOUT IT IN 1 SAMUEL 1:1–20.

DEVOTIONAL THOUGHT

Prayer is talking to God. You can talk to God any time, in any place! God promises to hear every prayer you pray. What can you pray about? Everything! Trust in God to hear and answer your prayer in the way He knows is best. Fill in the hearts below with your prayers, following the prompts beside each heart.

DEAR HEAVENLY FATHER,

I know You always hear my prayers. Thank You for listening to me. When I feel ignored or lonely, remind me that I can always talk to You. I am sorry for all the wrong I have done. Please forgive me and fill me with Your peace. In Jesus' name I pray. **AMEN.**

I LOVE YOU SO MUCH THAT I SENT MY SON TO DIE FOR YOU.

For God so loved the world, that He gave His only Son, that whoever believes in Him should not perish but have eternal life. **JOHN 3:16**

Even after Adam and Eve disobeyed God, bringing sin and death into the world, God kept loving them. He promised to send a Savior who would save all believers from eternal death. Jesus is the promised Savior!

READ ABOUT IT IN JOHN CHAPTERS 19 AND 20.

DEVOTIONAL THOUGHT

If you ever wonder about God's love for you, remember the words of John 3:16 and read again the account of Jesus' death on the cross and His resurrection from the grave. How much does God love you? So much that He gave His life for you so you can be with Him forever! Take some time to think about God's great love as you fill in the rest of this picture with tiny patterns and designs.

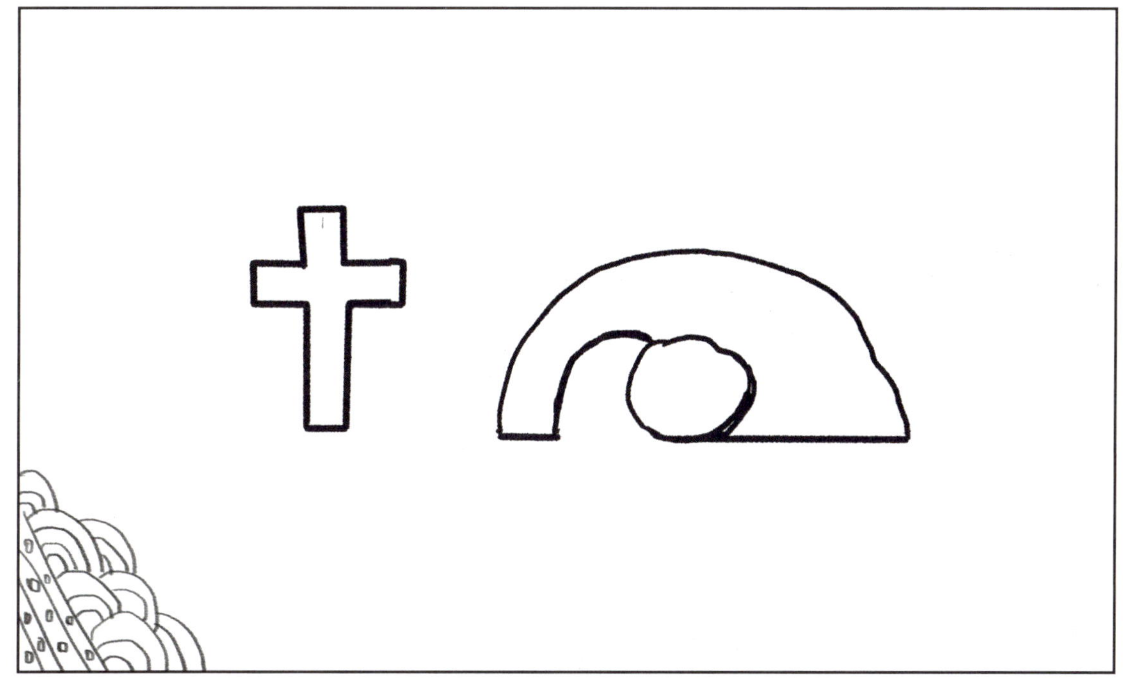

DEAR JESUS,

Thank You for dying and rising again to forgive my sin. When I start to think that I can be happy on my own and do what I want, remind me how much I need Your love and forgiveness. You are the only one who can make me truly happy, Jesus. In Your name I pray. **AMEN.**

YOU ARE MY BELOVED CHILD.

See what kind of love the Father has given to us, that we should be called children of God; and so we are. *1 JOHN 3:1*

When parents brought their children to Jesus for a blessing, the disciples tried to send them away. But Jesus invited the children into His arms, saying, "Let the children come to Me."

READ ABOUT IT IN MARK 10:13–16.

DEVOTIONAL THOUGHT

What does it mean to be a child of God? It means that you are loved and valued by the Creator of the universe—the one who created *you*! He has made you a member of His family, and you are precious to Him. As you color and decorate the word art below, remember who God has made you to be.

DEAR JESUS,

Thank You for blessing me and showing me that I am Your child. When I doubt my own worth and question my identity, remind me of Your blessings and the promise that I am Your child. Help me know that my worth is found in You. In Your name I pray. **AMEN.**

I WILL NEVER LEAVE YOU.

It is the Lord
who goes before you. He
will be with you; He will not leave you
or forsake you. Do not fear or be dismayed.

DEUTERONOMY 31:8

God chose Joshua to lead the Israelites into the Promised Land. "Be strong and courageous!" God told him, and then He gave Joshua a wonderful promise: "Just as I was with Moses, so I will be with you. I will not leave you or forsake you."

READ ABOUT IT IN JOSHUA 1:1–9.

DEVOTIONAL THOUGHT

God promised He would be with Joshua as he led God's people into the Promised Land. God promises to be with you too, no matter where you go. He will never leave you. Fill in the boxes below with the places you go: your home, school, church, neighborhood. Remember, God is with you every step of the way!

DEAR HEAVENLY FATHER,

Thank You for always being with me and promising never to leave me. When I feel alone and don't know where I am going, send Your Spirit to comfort me and remind me You are always near. Remind me that You will always go before me. In Jesus' name I pray. **AMEN.**

I GIVE YOU MY PEACE.

Peace I leave with you; My peace I give to you. Not as the world gives do I give to you. Let not your hearts be troubled, neither let them be afraid. **JOHN 14:27**

When Jesus told His disciples He would be leaving them soon, they got nervous. What would happen to Jesus? What would happen to *them*? But Jesus calmed them with a promise of peace—a special peace that only God can give.

READ ABOUT IT IN JOHN 14:18–31.

DEVOTIONAL THOUGHT

There are many symbols that have been used to describe peace. Create your own peace sign. Describe why you designed it that way. Remember that true peace comes only from God.

MY PEACE SYMBOL

DEAR JESUS,

You give peace that is better than anything in the whole world. Thank You for giving me that peace. When I am scared or troubled, give me Your peace and comfort me. Help me to remember that You are the only source of true peace. In Your name I pray. **AMEN.**

I WILL HELP YOU WHEN YOU ARE TEMPTED.

No temptation has overtaken you that is not common to man. God is faithful, and He will not let you be tempted beyond your ability, but with the temptation He will also provide the way of escape, that you may be able to endure it. *1 CORINTHIANS 10:13*

The devil came to test Jesus when He was hungry and tired. Three times, the devil tempted Jesus to sin and three times, Jesus spoke words of Scripture and rejected every temptation. Jesus kept God's Law perfectly and defeated the devil!

READ ABOUT IT IN MATTHEW 4:1–11.

DEVOTIONAL THOUGHT

The devil is constantly tempting us to sin, trying to get us to focus on the things the world says are good instead of trusting what God tells us is good. Keep your eyes on Jesus, and He will help you resist the temptations of the devil. Connect each colored set of dots to make an image that reminds us of Jesus. Decorate and color it in. Jesus promises to help when you are tempted—keep your eyes on Him!

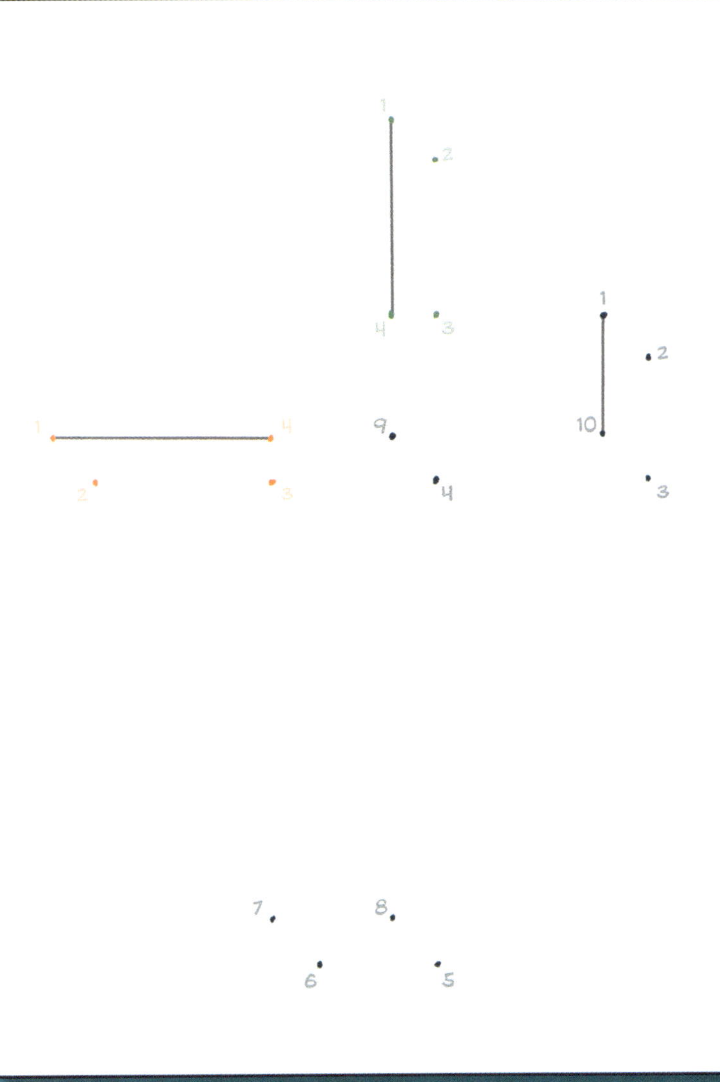

DEAR JESUS,

Thank You for strengthening me when I face temptation. When I am struggling to do what is right, help me remember that You know what it is like to be tempted. Send the Holy Spirit to help me resist temptation and do what is right. In Your holy name I pray. **AMEN.**

I AM THE WAY, THE TRUTH, AND THE LIFE.

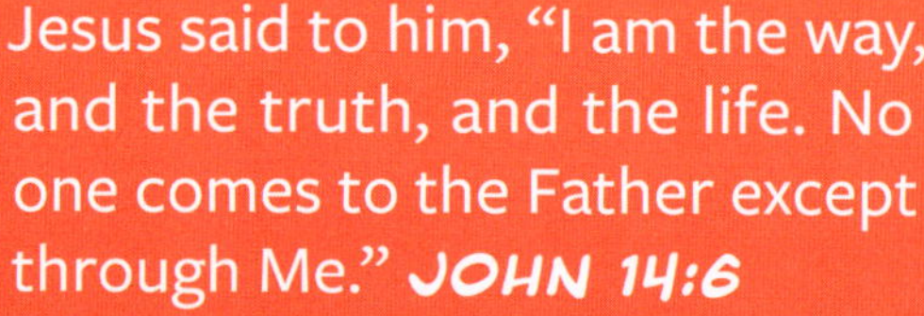

Jesus said to him, "I am the way, and the truth, and the life. No one comes to the Father except through Me." JOHN 14:6

Jesus met a woman who was spiritually lost. She was following a sinful path in life, and she was lonely and sad. Jesus offered the woman living water—the gift of the Holy Spirit, who creates faith and new life. Jesus is the way to eternal life.

READ ABOUT IT IN JOHN 4:1–42.

DEVOTIONAL THOUGHT

When you question or doubt your faith, Jesus reminds you that He is the only way. When the world tells you lies, He reminds you that He is the truth. When you despair or can't seem to find joy in this life, He reminds you that He is the life. All good things are found in Jesus. Make your own circle maze. Trace parts of the circles, adding lines and openings to make a path that leads to Jesus in the center.

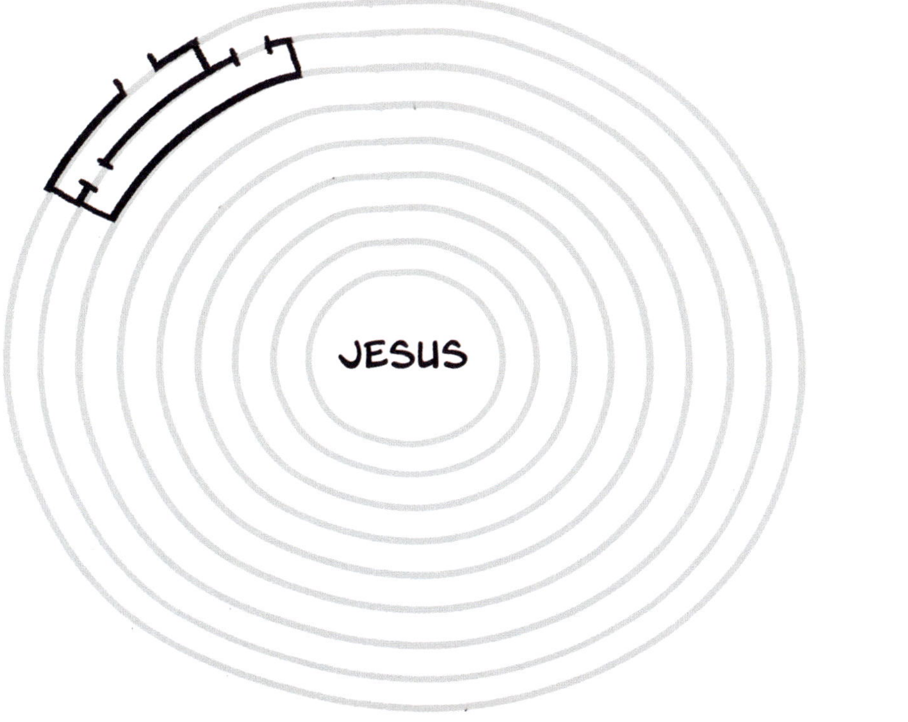

DEAR JESUS,

Thank You for being the way, the truth, and the life for all people. When I am lost, confused, or sad, please send Your Spirit to comfort me and remind me of Your words. Help me to always trust in You and in Your promises. In Your name I pray. **AMEN.**

I HAVE CALLED YOU BY NAME.

But now thus
says the LORD, He who
created you, O Jacob, He who formed
you, O Israel: "Fear not, for I have redeemed you;
I have called you by name, you are Mine." *ISAIAH 43:1*

One night as Samuel was sleeping, the Lord called out to him by name. Even though Samuel was just a boy at the time, God knew him and called him to be His special prophet.

READ ABOUT IT IN 1 SAMUEL 3:1–21.

DEVOTIONAL THOUGHT

You are one of eight billion people living in this world. You know what's amazing? God knows each of those eight billion people *by name*. He knows *you* by name. Even more amazing is that He knows everything about you, and He loves and cares for you. You are His, and He is yours. Write your name on the nametag below, then decorate it to make it uniquely yours.

HELLO,
MY NAME IS

GOD HAS CALLED ME
TO BE HIS OWN CHILD!

DEAR FATHER IN HEAVEN,

Thank You for calling me to be Yours. You called Samuel by name—remind me that You also know my name. When I feel like no one knows who I really am, help me know that You have chosen me and know everything about me. In Your name I pray. **AMEN.**

MY MERCY FOR YOU IS NEW EVERY DAY.

The steadfast love of the Lord never ceases; His mercies never come to an end; they are new every morning; great is Your faithfulness.

LAMENTATIONS 3:22–23

King David had done some terrible things. He sinned against God and hurt others. David was filled with guilt and confessed his sins to the Lord, trusting in God's forgiveness and mercy.

READ ABOUT IT IN PSALM 51:1–12.

DEVOTIONAL THOUGHT

When you mess up and sin, go to God and confess to Him what you have done. He has promised to show you mercy for Jesus' sake and forgive your sins. Your heavenly Father has a never-ending supply of new mercies to give you a fresh start every day! Draw your idea of a new day. In the clouds, write the blessings God gives you each new day.

DEAR HEAVENLY FATHER,

You have promised in Your Word that Your mercies are new every day. Please forgive me for all the wrongs I do and remind me of Your mercy and forgiveness. In Jesus' name I pray. ***AMEN.***

I LOVE YOU JUST THE WAY YOU ARE.

God shows His love for us in that while we were still sinners, Christ died for us.
ROMANS 5:8

There were not many Jews who liked Zacchaeus. In fact, most of them probably hated him. Zacchaeus was a tax collector, and tax collectors were known for taking lots more money than they should. But there was one person who still loved Zacchaeus, despite his bad reputation.

READ ABOUT IT IN LUKE 19:1–10.

DEVOTIONAL THOUGHT

You can't earn God's love—no one can! God the Father loves you because He made you, and you are His child. He forgives you because Jesus paid the punishment for all your sins. God's love is unconditional, and it is life-changing! Look in a mirror and draw yourself, then draw a heart around your picture. No matter what, you are loved by God!

I AM LOVED BY GOD

DEAR HEAVENLY FATHER,

Thank You for always loving me. When I think I can earn Your love, remind me of my sinfulness and Your forgiveness. Let the Holy Spirit work in me to love others as You have loved me. In Jesus' name I pray. **AMEN.**

I KNOW WHAT IS BEST FOR YOU.

The heart of man plans his way, but the LORD establishes his steps. ***PROVERBS 16:9***

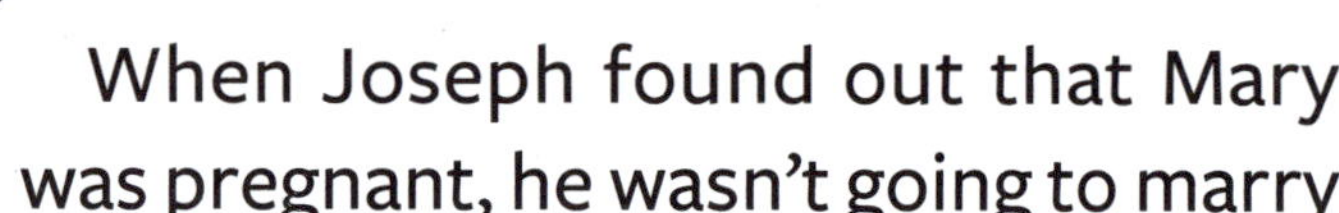

When Joseph found out that Mary was pregnant, he wasn't going to marry her. But God sent an angel to tell Joseph that the baby was the Savior of the world. Joseph listened to the angel, trusting that God's plans are best.

READ ABOUT IT IN MATTHEW 1:18–25.

DEVOTIONAL THOUGHT

God's plans are always best! Make beautiful designs or fun doodles in the footprints to remind you how God leads you to walk in His good ways.

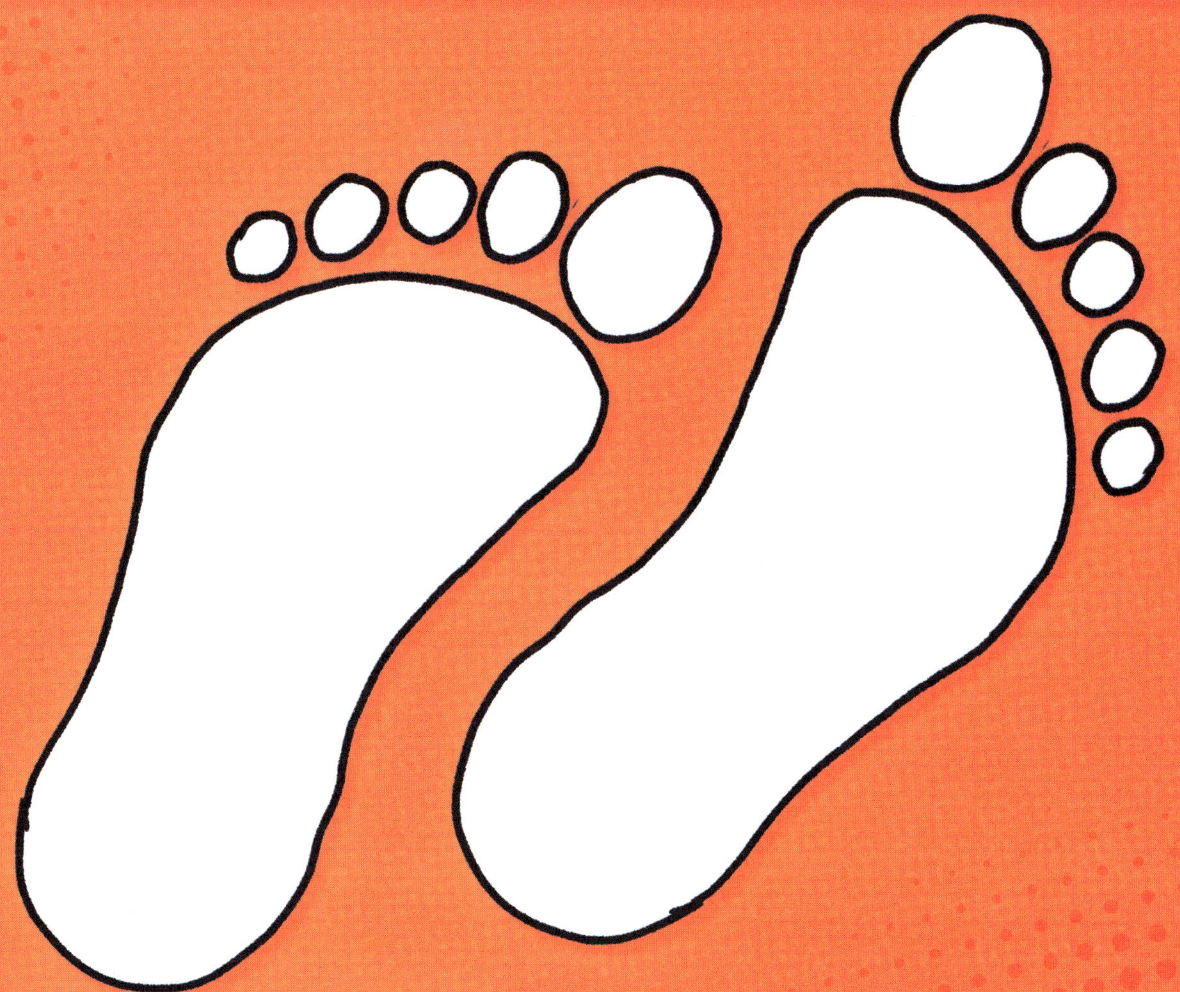

DEAR FATHER,

Thank You for sending Your very own Son to save the world. When I want to do things my way or start to think I know what is best, remind me that You created all things and You know what is best for each and every one of us. In Jesus' name I pray. **AMEN.**

I FORGIVE YOUR SINS.

If we confess our sins, He is faithful and just to forgive us our sins and to cleanse us from all unrighteousness. *1 JOHN 1:9*

Two criminals were next to Jesus' cross—one on the left and one on the right. One of the criminals made fun of Jesus, but the other admitted his sins and asked Jesus to have mercy on him. Jesus told him, "Today you will be with Me in paradise."

READ ABOUT IT IN LUKE 23:32–43.

DEVOTIONAL THOUGHT

There is no sin too big for Jesus to forgive. Write or draw some of your sins in the outline of the cross below. Then color over those sins with a red marker. Jesus has forgiven your sins and has given you the promise of eternal life!

DEAR JESUS,

You forgave the thief on the cross, and I know You forgive me too. Thank You for Your mercy and kindness. When I feel the guilt of all the bad things I have done, remind me that You still love me and that You have forgiven all my sins. In Your holy name I pray. **AMEN.**

I AM THE RESURRECTION AND THE LIFE.

Jesus said to her, "I am the resurrection and the life. Whoever believes in Me, though he die, yet shall he live, and everyone who lives and believes in Me shall never die."

JOHN 11:25-26

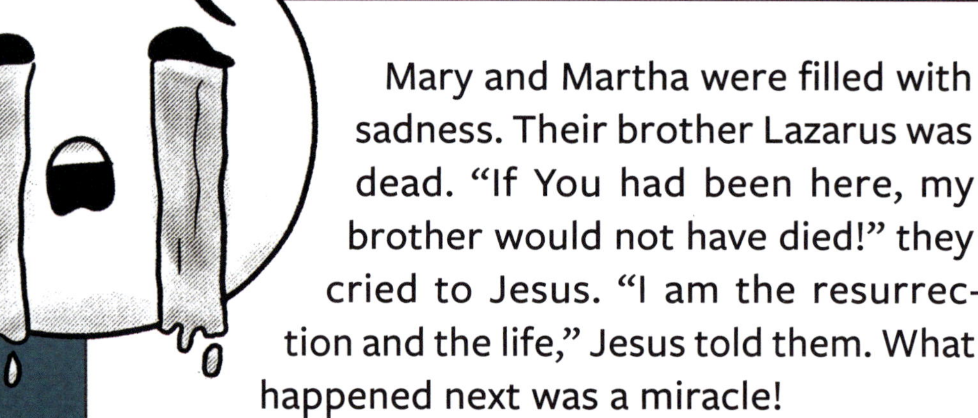

Mary and Martha were filled with sadness. Their brother Lazarus was dead. "If You had been here, my brother would not have died!" they cried to Jesus. "I am the resurrection and the life," Jesus told them. What happened next was a miracle!

READ ABOUT IT IN JOHN 11:1-44.

DEVOTIONAL THOUGHT

Jesus is God. That means He has power over all things, including death. He died on the cross to pay for our sins, but He didn't stay dead! Because Jesus rose, one day all believers will rise to eternal life! Draw trees, flowers, grass, and other living things around the empty tomb as a reminder that Jesus gives us new life!

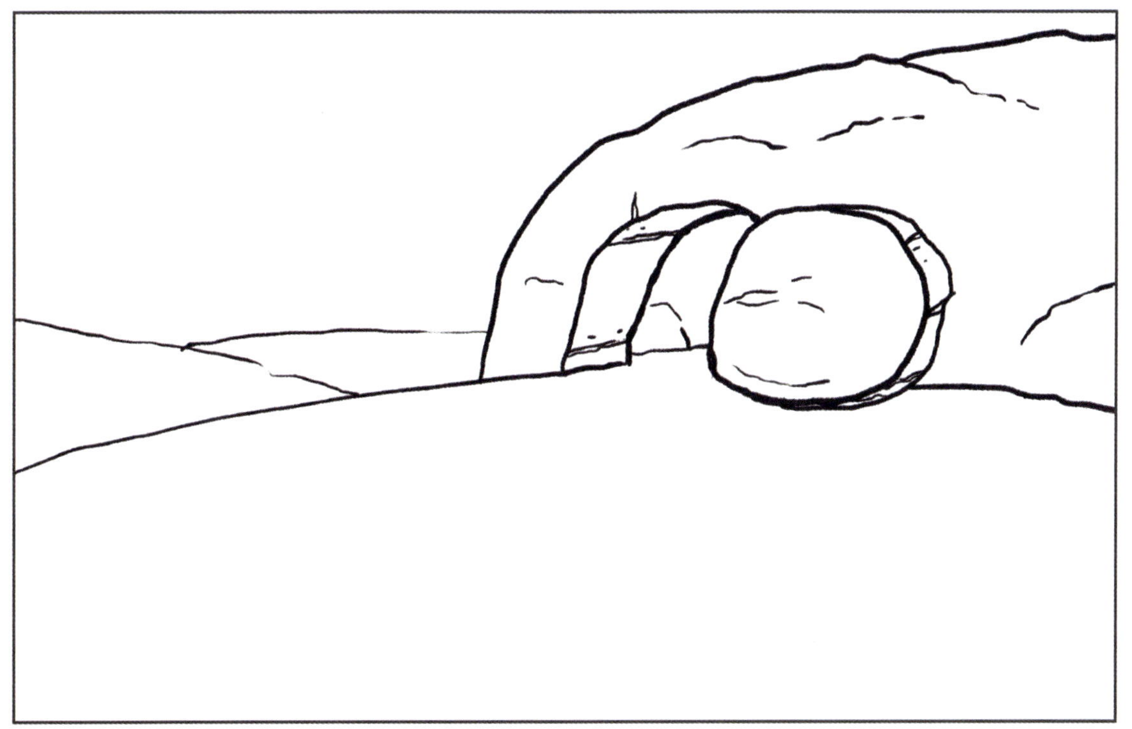

DEAR JESUS,

Thank You for promising to raise me and all believers to eternal life when You come again. When I fear death, remind me of Your power and that You are the resurrection and the life. Help me to always trust in You. In Your name I pray. **AMEN.**

I FILL YOU WITH JOY.

These things I have spoken to you, that My joy may be in you, and that your joy may be full. ***JOHN 15:11***

Wise Men from the East saw a special star in the sky, and they knew that a great king had been born. When the star led them to the place where Jesus was, they were filled with joy and they fell down and worshiped Him!

READ ABOUT IT IN MATTHEW 2:1–12.

DEVOTIONAL THOUGHT

Jesus is our King, the Savior whom God had promised to send to fix the broken world and turn our sadness into joy! Draw things in the gift boxes that bring you joy. These are all blessings from God. Jesus is the greatest gift of all!

DEAR HEAVENLY FATHER,

Thank You for sending Jesus to be my Savior. When I feel sad, send Your Spirit to bring me joy. Remind me of the Wise Men who saw the star. Help me to be like those Wise Men and find my joy in Your greatest gift, Jesus. In Jesus' name I pray. **AMEN.**

I WILL STRENGTHEN YOU.

But they who wait for the LORD shall renew their strength; they shall mount up with wings like eagles; they shall run and not be weary; they shall walk and not faint. ISAIAH 40:31

God's people were in danger. A man named Haman had a plan to destroy them. Esther knew that as the queen, she could ask the king to save her people, but she also knew that the king could choose not to listen and instead put her to death. What would she do?

READ ABOUT IT IN ESTHER 4:4–17.

DEVOTIONAL THOUGHT

God gave Esther the strength to talk to the king, and God's people were saved. God gives us strength to do the right thing too! He makes us strong, like a mighty eagle who soars high above the earth. Draw the wings of the eagle, then draw mountains, trees, and roads far below!

DEAR HEAVENLY FATHER,

Thank You for giving me faith in You. When I feel weak and helpless, please strengthen me and remind me of Your promises. Help me to be like Esther and do what is right even when I am scared. In Jesus' name I pray. **AMEN.**

I WILL COMFORT YOU.

Blessed
be the God and
Father of our Lord Jesus
Christ, the Father of mercies and God of
all comfort, who comforts us in all our affliction, so
that we may be able to comfort those who are in any affliction,
with the comfort with which we ourselves are comforted by God.

2 CORINTHIANS 1:3–4

Jesus knew all about the hurts and problems of the people who followed Him. He took the time to listen to their needs. In the Sermon on the Mount, Jesus encouraged and comforted the people by teaching them about the blessings that God gives to those who follow Him.

READ ABOUT IT IN MATTHEW 5:1–10.

DEVOTIONAL THOUGHT

How does God comfort you? What blessings does He give that help you when you are sad or anxious? Write or draw the blessings on the hillside below. Fill the hillside with flowers or other images that remind you of God's care and comfort for you.

DEAR LORD JESUS,

Thank You for comforting me in all my troubles. When I hurt or feel overwhelmed, send Your Spirit to be with me and comfort me. Remind me of the blessings You give that bring me comfort in my sadness. In Your name I pray. **AMEN.**

I REJOICE OVER YOU.

The LORD your God is in your midst, a mighty one who will save; He will rejoice over you with gladness; He will quiet you by His love; He will exult over you with loud singing.

ZEPHANIAH 3:17

The Pharisees didn't think that Jesus should hang around with tax collectors and other "sinners." So Jesus told them a story to help them understand: when a shepherd loses a sheep, he searches and searches until he finds it, and then he rejoices that the sheep is found!

READ ABOUT IT IN LUKE 15:1–7.

DEVOTIONAL THOUGHT

Have you ever thought about Jesus rejoicing over you? He does! Just as the shepherd shouted for joy when he found the one sheep who was lost, Jesus rejoices that you believe in Him. You are His precious sheep! Draw other sheep to join the one in the pasture. Jesus rejoices over all His sheep!

DEAR JESUS,

Thank You for rejoicing over me. I know I am Your child. Help me to rejoice because of what You have done for me. When I become lost in sin, bring me back to You so that we can rejoice together again. In Your name I pray. **AMEN.**

I WILL HELP YOU.

I lift up my
eyes to the hills. From
where does my help come? My help
comes from the LORD, who made heaven and
earth. He will not let your foot be moved; He who keeps you
will not slumber. *PSALM 121:1-3*

HELP!!!

When Bartimaeus, who was blind, heard that Jesus was passing by, he cried out to Him for help. "Be quiet!" the people around him scolded. But Bartimaeus kept calling out to Jesus. Jesus heard his cries for help, called Bartimaeus to Him, and gave him back his sight.

READ ABOUT IT IN MARK 10:46-52.

DEVOTIONAL THOUGHT

Bartimaeus believed Jesus could help him. We know Jesus will help us too, no matter what we need. Finish drawing the eyes. Draw some of the things Bartimaeus may have seen after Jesus restored his sight. We keep our eyes on Jesus, knowing He will help us!

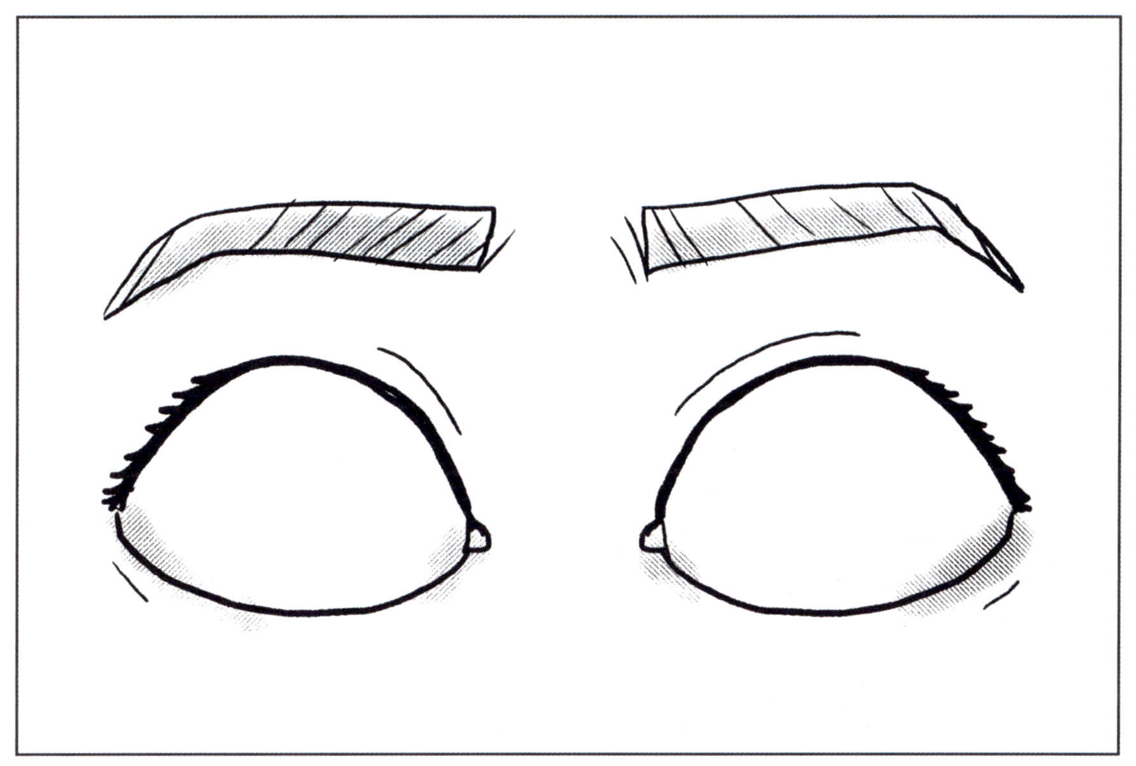

DEAR JESUS,

Thank You for Your promise to help me in every situation. Remind me that You hear every prayer, and You have the power to help. Guide me to help and care for others as You care for me. In Your powerful name I pray. **AMEN.**

I WILL GIVE YOU WHAT YOU NEED.

Therefore do not be anxious, saying, "What shall we eat?" or "What shall we drink?" or "What shall we wear?" For the Gentiles seek after all these things, and your heavenly Father knows that you need them all. But seek first the kingdom of God and His righteousness, and all these things will be added to you. ***MATTHEW 6:31–33***

The widow of Zarephath had just about given up. She had only enough flour and oil left to make bread for herself and her son one last time. Then the prophet Elijah showed up, asking for food and giving her God's promise that the flour and oil would not run out until the drought was over.

READ ABOUT IT IN 1 KINGS 17:7–16.

DEVOTIONAL THOUGHT

We sometimes worry that we won't get everything we need (or think we need). But God knows better than we do what our needs are! We can trust Him to take care of us. Look at the colored shapes below. Add lines and shapes to them to create some of the things God provides for us.

DEAR FATHER IN HEAVEN,

Thank You for promising to give me all that I need. When I lack something, please provide for me in the way that You see fit. Guide me to help others with their needs too. In Jesus' name I pray. ***AMEN.***

I HAVE SAVED YOU.

For by grace
you have been saved
through faith. And this is not your own
doing; it is the gift of God, not a result of works,
so that no one may boast. *EPHESIANS 2:8–9*

Rahab was a foreigner who had lived a sinful life. But she hid two Israelite spies from the king, saving their lives. Why? She had heard about the amazing things the one true God had done, and the Holy Spirit worked in her heart to believe in Him. God then saved her family from destruction.

READ ABOUT IT IN JOSHUA 2:1–24.

DEVOTIONAL THOUGHT

We try to be kind to others, obey our parents, and do the right thing, but we end up messing up sometimes. When we feel the guilt of our sin, Jesus invites us to look to Him. He took all our sins on Himself at the cross so that we can have forgiveness and the gift of eternal life. Draw a cross to connect the two cliffs. Jesus made a way for us to live forever with Him!

DEAR JESUS,

When I feel the weight of my sin, remind me of Your forgiveness and Your promise to save me. Thank You for giving me the gift of eternal life. In Your holy name I pray. **AMEN.**

I AM MAKING YOU INTO A NEW CREATION.

Therefore, if anyone is in Christ, he is a new creation. The old has passed away; behold, the new has come. ***2 CORINTHIANS 5:17***

No one liked tax collectors. They worked for the Roman government and often took more taxes than they should, pocketing the change. Why in the world would Jesus call Matthew, the tax collector, to follow Him?

READ ABOUT IT IN MATTHEW 9:9–13.

DEVOTIONAL THOUGHT

We are sinners, just like Matthew and all people. We can't do anything good on our own. But Jesus has made us new through the work of the Holy Spirit. The Spirit works in your life to help you live in a way that is pleasing to Him. Decorate and color the butterfly wings to show how God has made you a beautiful new creation.

DEAR HEAVENLY FATHER,

Thank You for making me new and beautiful through the work of the Holy Spirit. Help me live a new life in You. In Jesus' name I pray. **AMEN.**

I WILL DESTROY PAIN AND DEATH FOREVER.

He will wipe
away every tear from
their eyes, and death shall be no more,
neither shall there be mourning, nor crying, nor
pain anymore, for the former things have passed away.

REVELATION 21:4

"Please come," a father begged Jesus, "my little girl is dying." On the way, a woman who had been in pain for twelve years saw Jesus and touched the edge of His cloak, believing Jesus would heal her. Jesus healed the woman, but when He got to the house, the girl had died. Jesus took her by the hand and raised her back to life!

READ ABOUT IT IN MARK 5:21–43.

DEVOTIONAL THOUGHT

Jesus has power over all things, including sickness and death. Use a pencil to write on the hands some things that hurt us and make us sad. Then use lots of colors to cover over the words. One day, Jesus will destroy sin and death forever and make all things beautiful and new!

DEAR HEAVENLY FATHER,

When I hurt or fear death, help me remember that You have power over all things. Remind me that one day, You will destroy pain and death forever, and I will live in perfect happiness with You. In Your name I pray. **AMEN.**

I WILL MAKE ALL THINGS NEW.

Then I saw a new heaven and a new earth, for the first heaven and the first earth had passed away, and the sea was no more.

REVELATION 21:1

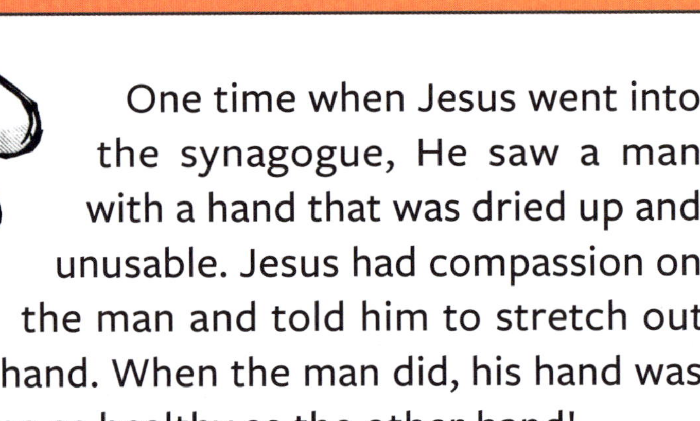

One time when Jesus went into the synagogue, He saw a man with a hand that was dried up and unusable. Jesus had compassion on the man and told him to stretch out his hand. When the man did, his hand was restored and became as healthy as the other hand!

READ ABOUT IT IN MATTHEW 12:9–13.

DEVOTIONAL THOUGHT

When God created the world, everything was perfect. Sin ruined God's perfect world, so now things get sick and broken. Jesus came to fix the broken world. He showed this by healing people when He lived on earth. One day, Jesus will make everything new, so the world will be perfect once again! Draw your idea of the perfect new heavens and earth. We don't know exactly what it will be like, but we know it will be wonderful!

DEAR JESUS,

Thank You for Your promise of a new heaven and a new earth. When I feel broken and ashamed of who I am, remind me that You make me new. Let Your Spirit work in me to help me become more like You. In Your name I pray. ***AMEN.***

MY WORD IS TRUE.

If you abide in
My word, you are truly My
disciples, and you will know the truth,
and the truth will set you free. *JOHN 8:31–32*

Some of the people following Jesus didn't believe what He was saying to them. Some even turned away from Him. So Jesus asked His disciples if they would leave Him too. Peter answered, "Lord, to whom shall we go? You have the words of eternal life."

READ ABOUT IT IN JOHN 6:63–69.

DEVOTIONAL THOUGHT

The words we read and hear in the Bible aren't always easy to understand and believe. The world's message is sometimes so different from God's message. But one thing is for sure: God's Word is true, and only God's Word gives life—eternal life. Write some of your favorite words of God below on the pages of the Bible.

DEAR HEAVENLY FATHER,

Thank You for the gift of Your true and holy Word. When I doubt what I read or hear, remind me that all You have spoken is true and always will be. Help me to trust in You and in Your promises. In Jesus' name I pray. **AMEN.**

NOTHING CAN SEPARATE YOU FROM ME.

For I am sure that neither death nor life, nor angels nor rulers, nor things present nor things to come, nor powers, nor height nor depth, nor anything else in all creation, will be able to separate us from the love of God in Christ Jesus our Lord. **ROMANS 8:38–39**

When Jesus died on the cross, the disciples felt lost and afraid. Their master and friend was gone—or so they thought. Then Jesus appeared to them, alive! He opened their minds to understand that He is the Savior who had been promised from the time of Adam and Eve. Jesus overcame death and the devil so that all who believe in Him will have forgiveness of sins and eternal life.

READ ABOUT IT IN LUKE 24:36–53.

DEVOTIONAL THOUGHT

When you feel lost or alone, remember Jesus is with you and nothing can separate you from Him. He gives you special people who remind you of His love for you. Draw a picture of yourself and someone who shares God's love with you. Then draw a picture of yourself and Jesus, your forever friend and Savior.

DEAR JESUS,

I am so thankful that nothing can separate me from Your love. When I feel far away from You and unworthy of Your love, remind me that Your forgiveness is a gift and You will always love me. Teach me that nothing can separate me from Your love. In Your name I pray. **AMEN.**

I AM PREPARING A PLACE FOR YOU IN HEAVEN.

In My Father's house are many rooms. If it were not so, would I have told you that I go to prepare a place for you? And if I go and prepare a place for you, I will come again and will take you to Myself, that where I am you may be also. **JOHN 14:2–3**

When Jesus comes again, He will make everything new. God gave the apostle John a vision of the new heaven and earth, where God will dwell with His people forever. He will forever be their God, and they will forever be His people, and there will be no more sadness, pain, or death.

READ ABOUT IT IN REVELATION 21:1–4.

DEVOTIONAL THOUGHT

What will the new heavens and earth be like? We don't know everything, but we do know that we will live with God forever, in perfect peace and happiness! Draw a picture of your idea of the perfect room below. What God has in store for His people is so much better than anything we could imagine!

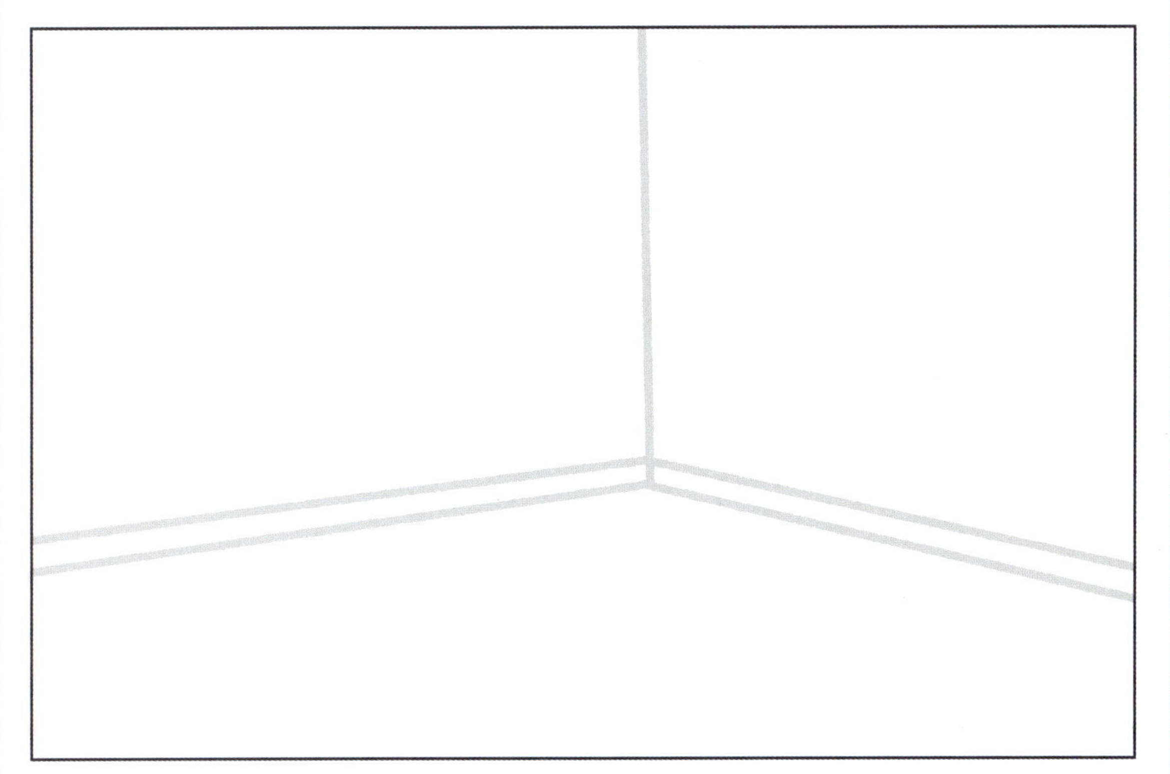

DEAR FATHER,

Thank You for preparing a place for me in heaven. When I worry about the future or wonder about heaven, remind me of Your promise to one day take me to be with You forever, where I will live in perfect joy. In Your name I pray. **AMEN.**

I AM ALL YOU TRULY NEED.

Whom have I in heaven but You? And there is nothing on earth that I desire besides You. My flesh and my heart may fail, but God is the strength of my heart and my portion forever.

PSALM 73:25–26

When Jesus came to visit His friends Mary and Martha, Martha scurried around the house, cleaning and preparing food while Mary sat at Jesus' feet and listened to Him. Martha got upset—why wasn't Mary helping her? But Jesus reminded her that He is the one thing that is necessary.

READ ABOUT IT IN LUKE 10:38–42.

DEVOTIONAL THOUGHT

We seem to have many needs and even more things that we want, but there is only one thing we truly need: faith in Jesus Christ. Jesus is our loving Savior and He gives us all that we need, not just for this life but for life eternal with Him. Draw some of your needs around the cross. Jesus has taken care of your greatest need: forgiveness.

DEAR JESUS,

Thank You for being all that I need. When I become worried about all the things I think I need, remind me of Your promises to provide for me. Help me look to You as the one thing that is necessary. In Your name I pray. **AMEN.**

I AM YOUR REFUGE AND STRENGTH.

PSALM 46:1

I WILL PROTECT YOU.

PSALM 32:7

I AM YOUR ROCK AND DELIVERER.

PSALM 18:2

I MAKE YOU WISE.

JAMES 1:5

I NEVER LIE.

NUMBERS 23:19

I AM WITH YOU ALWAYS.

MATTHEW 28:20

I AM SLOW TO ANGER.

PSALM 103:8

I AM YOUR GOOD SHEPHERD.

JOHN 10:11

I HAVE GIVEN YOU ETERNAL LIFE.

1 JOHN 5:11–13

I HAVE OVERCOME THE WORLD.

JOHN 16:33

NOTES

NOTES

I AM YOUR LIGHT AND SALVATION.

PSALM 27:1

I WILL GUIDE YOU.

PROVERBS 3:5-6

I GIVE YOU EVERY GOOD THING.

PSALM 103:2-4

I AM NEAR TO YOU.

PSALM 145:18-19

I WILL TEACH YOU THE WAY TO GO.

PSALM 32:8

I AM ON YOUR SIDE.

PSALM 118:6-7

I WILL GIVE YOU REST.

MATTHEW 11:28

I HAVE CHOSEN YOU.

JOHN 15:16

I HAVE MADE YOU A LIGHT TO SHINE MY LOVE.

MATTHEW 5:14-16

MY LOVE IS FOR ALL PEOPLE.

2 PETER 3:9

PROMISE FINDER

SCRIPTURE FINDER

SCRIPTURE FINDER [CON'T]